JAMES FRITZ

James Fritz's other plays include *Parliament Square* (winner of the Judges' Award at the Bruntwood Prize for Playwriting; Royal Exchange Theatre, Manchester/Bush Theatre, London); *The Fall* (National Youth Theatre at Finborough Theatre); *Ross & Rachel* (MOTOR at Assembly George Square, Edinburgh Festival Fringe/59E59 Theaters, New York); *Four Minutes Twelve Seconds* (runner-up of Soho Theatre's 2013 Verity Bargate Award, nominated for an Olivier Award; Hampstead Theatre Downstairs) and *Lines* (Rosemary Branch Theatre).

James Fritz

COMMENT IS FREE
& START SWIMMING

Two Plays

NICK HERN BOOKS
London
www.nickhernbooks.co.uk

A Nick Hern Book

Comment Is Free & Start Swimming first published in Great Britain as a paperback original in 2017 by Nick Hern Books Limited, The Glasshouse, 49a Goldhawk Road, London W12 8QP

Cover image: Andrey_Kuzmin/Shutterstock.com

Designed and typeset by Nick Hern Books, London
Printed in Great Britain by Mimeo Ltd, Huntingdon, Cambridgeshire PE29 6XX

A CIP catalogue record for this book is available from the British Library

ISBN 978 1 84842 707 5

Introduction

It makes me very happy to see these two plays side by side.

Comment Is Free started life at Old Vic New Voices in June 2015, in a staged reading directed by Kate Hewitt and produced by Martha Rose Wilson. In the audience was Becky Ripley, an incredibly talented young radio producer who saw the potential for the play to work as an audio drama. Working closely with Becky I rewrote the text with radio in mind, and the play was broadcast on BBC Radio 4 in October 2016.

If you can find a version of the original radio production lurking somewhere on the internet it's worth having a listen, not least to imagine the long, long hours Becky must have spent in the editing room. Understanding that the feeling of the play's 'noise' is as crucial as its content, she spliced together a hundred different crowdsourced voices who delivered a mixture of written and improvised lines based on the text. The effect was noisy and disorientating in exactly the right way. Anyone thinking about performing this play on stage should feel free to do the same if they so wish – so long as the beats of the story are hit, it's more important that the noise feels exciting, realistic and terrifying than particularly faithful to the text.

Start Swimming was made incredibly quickly in the spring of 2017 with director Ola Ince and Young Vic Taking Part. Tasked with responding to Paul Mason's performance and book *Why It's Kicking Off Everywhere* (which documented the successes and failures of the various protests and revolutions of 2011), Ola and I worked with a group of twelve young people from Lambeth and Southwark to create a new piece that would transfer from the Young Vic to the Edinburgh Fringe. Our aim was to make something that would articulate how our cast felt about growing up marginalised in a major city during a time of incredible political upheaval.

We decided early on to make something that wasn't specific to any one voice or story in the room, but instead communicated their widely shared feelings of frustration, confusion, anger and powerlessness. This led to the text's bare, repetitive structure, which in rehearsals (thanks to Ola's input) was blended with a binary yes/no that would often reset proceedings when the wrong answer was given.

In Ola's original production – which staged the text in a sort of hellish gameshow, with the cast elevated on light-up boxes that would choose participants at random – the *yes*'s (Y) were marked by the ding of a bell, the *no*'s (X) by a buzzer which gave an electric shock to our committed actors. The effect was exhausting to watch in the best possible way, and the cast were some of the most inspiring, talented people I've had the pleasure to work with. Each of them took the offer given to them by the play's blankness and ran with it, stamping their own authority and identity over every word.

I'm excited to discover how those same Ys and Xs might be interpreted differently in the future, and how a new company's voices and experiences might change the meaning of *Start Swimming* in ways I can't imagine.

These two very different texts started life on the same street in London. Their first drafts were written about two years apart – two years in which it felt, and still feels, that the whole world turned upside down. Both attempted to capture a snapshot of this turbulent period. And both represent records of the first time I worked with brand new collaborators in a brand new way.

I hope you find them interesting.

James Fritz
October 2017

COMMENT IS FREE

Acknowledgements

With thanks to Alex Ferris and all at Old Vic New Voices, and Kate Hewitt, Martha Rose Wilson and the wonderful cast of our reading.

And Becky. Here's to making lots more noise together.

J.F.

This version of *Comment Is Free* was first broadcast on BBC Radio 4 on 5 October, 2016, with the following cast:

HILARY	Rachael Stirling
BEN	Tobias Menzies
EMMA WATKINS	Alice Kirk
POLICE OFFICER	Alison Belbin
EDITOR	Jolyon Jenkins
Director, Producer & Dramaturg	Becky Ripley

The news was read by Neil Nunes, Susan Rae, Zeb Soanes and Ritula Shah, with Jonathan Dimbleby hosting *Any Questions*.

'The Noise' was voiced by Natasha Cowley, Luke MacGregor, Clare Perkins and Gavi Singh Chera, alongside hundreds of crowdsourced contributors from across the country.

Note on Text

This is a text featuring hundreds of voices.

It should feel noisy – things should overlap, and not everything needs to be heard.

A line with no full stop at the end indicates an unfinished thought.

A dash at the end of a line indicates an interruption.

The journalist and political commentator
Alistair Cooper today sparked controversy –

Alistair Cooper/Alistair Cooper said/I hate
Alistair Cooper/I hate Alistair Cooper so much.
What's he said now?
Awful views. Awful man.
God I hate Alistair Cooper.

ALISTAIR   Hello, you've reached Alistair Cooper. I'm
                  not available right now but please leave me
                  a message and I'll get back to you.

HILARY   Alistair it's me. Can you pick something up
                  on your way home, I'm going late at work
                  again sorry love you bye.

Alistair Cooper and wife
Alistair Cooper, wife alongside him
Alistair Cooper's wife Hilary sports gorgeous
halterneck dress as she attends
Alistair Cooper's wife Hilary looks stylish
alongside her husband as he collects
Not hard to see why she married him is it?
She doesn't need his money, she's posher than
he is.
She's a QC apparently.
If she was my barrister I'd question her
judgement.
Alistair Cooper pictured with his wife Hilary
and their two-year-old daughter Agnes.
That poor child.
Imagine having Alistair Cooper as a father.
Oh god he's spawned.
People like him shouldn't be allowed kids.

ALISTAIR   Hello, you've reached Alistair Cooper. I'm
                  not available right now but please leave me
                  a message and I'll get back to you.

HILARY   Hiya it's me just to remind you Agnes has
                        her vaccination appointment but I'm having
                        lunch with my brother so can't take her. Love
                        you bye.

                        Alistair Cooper today sparked outrage with
                        fresh comments on
                        Comments on immigration
                        After referring to union leader Ken McNeil as
                        a cockroach
                        Cooper, appearing on The Daily Politics
                        argued that
                        Have you seen this?
                        Have you seen what Cooper's said this time?

JONATHAN DIMBLEBY
                        Hello and welcome to *Any Questions* from the
                        Radio Theatre in Broadcasting House,
                        London. On our panel this week is political
                        commentator Alistair Cooper

                        Not him again.
                        How can the BBC give a platform to a moron
                        like him.
                        He's a carbuncle on the backside of civilised
                        society and he needs to be removed
                        permanently.
                        Everybody hates you Alistair Cooper so just
                        hurry up and die.

JONATHAN DIMBLEBY
                        Alistair Cooper – Your response?

                        Alistair Cooper's latest comments have
                        sparked outrage on social media with
                        'ShutUpAlistair' trending for a large part of
                        the day.
                        ShutUpAlistair.
                        Hahaha love that ShutUpAlistair's trending
                        worldwide.
                        ShutUpAlistair/ShutUpAlistair/ShutUpAlistair
                        ShutUpAlistair I hate you. Now go away.

BEN   Heard Alistair on the radio.

HILARY	Was he good?
BEN	You didn't listen?
HILARY	Never do.
BEN	He really went for it.
HILARY	Always does.
BEN	He's getting worse. You really didn't listen? Some of the language he used –
HILARY	Why do you listen if he annoys you so much?
BEN	A lot of people are very upset.
HILARY	Oh they're always upset about something.
BEN	Maybe you should talk to him. Get him to tone things down. It's getting a bit out of hand.
HILARY	Don't be so dramatic.
BEN	I'm your brother.
HILARY	So.
BEN	So I'm worried about you. People are really angry.
HILARY	Alistair's been saying stuff like this for years. It's never bothered you before. What's this really about?
BEN	When I tell people he's my brother-in-law they. There's a look I get a look.
HILARY	What sort of look? Your lefty mates.
BEN	Yes but not just them. Strangers. People you meet.
	I was on a date last week and it was all going really well right up until I said that my sister was married to Alistair Cooper. After that he couldn't wait to get out of there.
HILARY	I'm sure Alistair's going to be devastated he's interfering with your love life.

BEN   Doesn't it get to you? How much people
                   hate him?

HILARY   Of course not. Never has. Alistair doesn't care
                   what people think of him and neither do I.
                   There's always been two Alistairs. You know
                   that. The real guy at home and the pantomime
                   villain. At home he's a great dad, a wonderful
                   husband and just about my favourite person
                   on the planet. They can hate the panto version
                   all they like.

                   I hate Alistair Cooper.
                   I hate Alistair Cooper.
                   I hate Alistair Cooper and everything he
                   stands for.

                   I quite like Alistair Cooper. I think he
                   articulates what a lot of the country is feeling.

                   Hi I don't know you at all but just to say if you
                   think Alistair Cooper is anything other than
                   a toff waste of space then you're a terrible
                   person.

                   Twenty-one Things Alistair Cooper said that
                   are just plain wrong.
                   Take our quiz. Who said this, Alistair or Adolf?
                   Twenty-two pieces of ham that look like
                   Alistair Cooper.
                   Bet he was bullied at school and now he's
                   taking it out on the country.

                   Why don't you ShutUpAlistair and leave us
                   in peace.
                   ShutUpAlistair.
                   Seriously, I don't usually say this but people
                   like him should be strung up.
                   Alistair Cooper's rhetoric is dangerous and
                   needs to be stopped.
                   The more people like Alistair Cooper are
                   allowed to denigrate the working class, the
                   more our country will feel divided.

*I'm with you mate put a bullet in the back of
their heads!*
Sign this petition ha ha!
*A petition asking the government to deport the
journalist Alistair Cooper has reached almost
three hundred thousand signatures in just
under a month.*
Yes!
Can we deport him to the bottom of the sea?

ALISTAIR   Hello, you've reached Alistair Cooper. I'm
not available right now but please leave me
a message and I'll get back to you.

HILARY   Alistair. It's me. If you haven't been deported
yet can you pick up some milk on your way
home I'm working late again. Oh and some
basil. See you soon love you bye.

*The controversial columnist Alistair Cooper
has once again sparked outrage.*
*How can anyone from his background talk
about inequality with a straight face.*
Posho.
Rich, arrogant man.
Don't give him the oxygen of publicity.
Don't give him oxygen full stop.

*Guys can we please stop mentioning Alistair
Cooper's name, it's exactly what he wants.*
Love how you just named him.
*Someone needs to silence Alistair Cooper
fast. The longer he is allowed to spout his
venom the more people will be hurt by the
intolerance and hatred he inspires.*

ALISTAIR   Hello, you've reached Alistair Cooper. I'm
not available right now but please leave me
a message and I'll get back to you.

HILARY   Hiya, I'm still at the office but I just wanted
to wish you good luck tonight. Remember to
talk slowly. And don't do that smirky thing
you do. Love you.

I swear Alistair Cooper is on Question Time
every week.
Why is he always smirking?
Insert Alistair Cooper joke here.
His face is like a ham. Hamface.
He's a bag of meat with a head made of
sausage.
Think Alistair Cooper's human suit is
malfunctioning.
Makes me want to vomit.
Hate him/I hate him.

Gonna murder you and your wife slowly and
then drown your daughter.

Alistair Cooper today posted a defiant
message in response to threats made on
social media.
Police are investigating threats made towards
Oh come on. Bit of an overreaction.
Obviously I don't condone comments like that
but Alistair Cooper does a lot more harm
every day of his life.
It's one isolated weirdo.
World's smallest violin.
Someone like him can't say what they like and
then whine when other people do the same.

BEN	Mum was worried. She wanted me to talk to you. The threats against Alistair –
HILARY	Gets them all the time.
BEN	The things they're saying.
HILARY	He finds it funny.
BEN	Funny?
HILARY	We both do. The police say it's nothing to worry about. Think he's enjoying the attention to be honest.
BEN	Well that doesn't surprise me. Mum's worried about you.

HILARY   Mum's worried about what people are saying
                round the village. You both need to ignore it.
                Trust me, it's all just noise.

                Alistair Cooper once again/Alistair
                Cooper/Alistair Cooper/Worst person
                ever/Awful man/I just wanna shut him up any
                way I can.
                ShutUpAlistair/I'm not usually in favour of
                assassination but
                Put an end to him.
                He's evil.
                Hateful man.
                Everything he says is poison.
                Alistair/Alistair Cooper/Alistair Cooper I/
                I hate Alistair Cooper/Hate him/Shut up/
                Alistair Cooper needs to/Cooper/Cooper/
                Cooper/Cooper/Alistair
                Hate him/Hate him/Shut up/Shut up/Shut up

                SHUT. UP.

POLICE OFFICER
                Ms Cooper?

HILARY   Yes.

POLICE OFFICER
                My name is Detective Constable Pinner and
                this is Police Constable Houghton. We need to
                talk to you about your husband. Is it alright if
                we come in?

HILARY   Yes.
                What's
                What's going on?

                Breaking news:
                The journalist and commentator Alistair
                Cooper has been found dead.
                Breaking news:

Breaking news:
Oh my god
And we've got some rather shocking breaking
news to bring you just
Holy shit
Oh wow
Oh my god
Breaking news:
Alistair Cooper
Alistair Cooper, political commentator and
former editor of
Alistair Cooper has died.
Has been found dead.
Dead.
Been found dead outside his Hampstead
home.
Have you seen this?
Seen this? Alistair Cooper's dead.
Alistair Cooper has been found dead outside
his Hampstead flat.

Wahey! Maybe there is a God.
Dad! You can't say that.
His poor family.
Never liked him much.

HILARY   I'm sorry. I.
                I don't understand.

POLICE OFFICER
                We're just trying to establish a timeline of
                events.

HILARY   I. I don't know I. Spoke to him about
                ten-thirty I. We said goodnight.

POLICE OFFICER
                And you were here the whole night?

HILARY   Yes. I. My daughter's upstairs.

POLICE OFFICER
                Can you think of anyone that might have
                wished harm on your husband?

Alistair Cooper found dead this morning.
Police are
More to follow.
Breaking/Breaking/Breaking/Ali/Alistair
Cooper/Ohmygod/Can't believe it/Knew
someone would/You're not gonna believe
More to follow.
Horrible thing.
What a terrible thing.
Oh my god how awful.
I didn't like the man but this is awful.
Never liked the man but this is terrible.
What a dreadful thing to have happened.
Didn't agree with his politics but I never
thought that he deserved this.
Never agreed with the man but that's just
Would never have wished anything like this on
the man.
Can't believe it.
What is wrong with this country?
Yet more evidence that our country is broken.
I didn't agree with his politics but
Whether or not you agreed with his politics.
Whether you thought he was right or not.
Whether you liked him or not.
Whether you thought he could be a vicious
bastard.
Whether you liked or loathed him.
Whether you
Whether or not you
Nobody deserves this.
Nobody deserves this.
He doesn't deserve this.
Nobody deserves this.

POLICE OFFICER

Someone will be around to talk to you
tomorrow. Have you got somebody you
can call?

HILARY   My. My brother. Ben.

POLICE OFFICER

> By now the media will have picked up the story. If you can, try and stay away from the television, the internet. We'll keep you abreast of everything that's going on.

> *Well.*
> *Well.*
> *Wonder what?*
> *What happened?*
> *How did he die does it say?*
> *Outside his home.*
> *We'll bring you more when we*
> *Reporting from the scene is*
> *Who the hell is Alistair Cooper?*
> *Looks like Alistair Cooper finally went too far.*
> *Finally went too far did he.*
> *That's what happens if you keep pushing people.*
> *I'm sorry to say it but it's hardly a surprise is it.*
> *Don't want to sound insensitive but this shows what happens when you try and make people hate you.*

BEN   I can't believe it.

HILARY   They don't know what happened.

BEN   The news alert on my phone went off and I just. How's Agnes?

HILARY   They need somebody to identify the body. I don't think I can

BEN   Of course. Just tell me where I need to go.

HILARY   I don't know what to do. I don't know what I'm supposed to do.

> *As far as the cause of death goes, nothing has been confirmed yet although*
> *We're still waiting to hear exactly what the cause of death was although neighbours are*

talking about a lot of blood and it's hard to
look beyond an attack.
My mate works for the Standard, *he just text*
to say Alistair Cooper was stabbed.
Murdered/has been/stab wounds/suspicious
circumstances/possibly murdered/suspects are

HILARY   He was staying in the flat in town. Had an
early TV interview this morning. A neighbour
found him but.
There was nothing they could –

BEN   Here. Drink this.

HILARY   Agnes is upstairs. I haven't told her yet.
I don't know how. She's two years old. How
do I explain this to her?

BEN   I don't know.

HILARY   The news. She's going to see the news.
Online. They're saying
Saying all sorts of things.

BEN   You shouldn't read all that.

HILARY   Theories about what happened.
I don't know what to believe.

BEN   Don't pay attention to any of that. Just focus
on Agnes for now eh?

Police
Police are
The murder of Alistair Cooper
Looking for any information that might
What happened?
Wonder what happened?
Oh my god he was murdered.
Who was?
Alistair Cooper.
Who's Alistair Cooper?
How tragic.
What a tragedy.

HILARY	My phone keeps going off. Everyone already knows. Our friends. His family. Work.
BEN	The whole country knows Hil.
HILARY	But it should be me that breaks the news to them. Shouldn't it? That's my job. Oh my god work I need to call work
BEN	Sit down.
HILARY	I've got so much I need to get done and And I keep thinking. He must've. Must've been so scared.
BEN	I know. Shhh. It's alright. It's alright.
HILARY	How can this have happened I don't understand. I need to understand.

I just hope that people don't use this to make him some sort of martyr.
Obviously politically motivated.
Died for what he believed in.
Died saying what he thought.
Can we please stop politicising a man's death before the body's cold thank you.

Still waiting for the facts to come in.
We don't even know if it was murder.
Heard he was stabbed.
They're saying he was stabbed.
We're hearing unconfirmed rumours that Alistair Cooper was stabbed.
Let's try and wait for the facts before we start jumping to conclusions shall we?
We don't know what happened so let's just hold off until we do.

HILARY	Hi, thanks for ringing.

Police are still carrying out inquiries into the murder of Alistair Cooper.

*A video of Alistair Cooper circulating. Taken
by a neighbour.
Footage of Alistair Cooper's corpse taken by
a neighbour.*

HILARY   Hi thanks for calling.

*Warning. Some viewers may find these images
disturbing.*

HILARY   So lovely of you to call yes it's all a bit of
a shock.

*Shocking footage of the moment Alistair
Cooper's body was found.*

HILARY   Thank you, that means a lot. We're okay. Still
trying to process.
I'm sorry. Video? What video?

*Have you seen the video of Alistair Cooper's
body?
So much blood.
Can't believe it.
We really shouldn't be watching this.
Have you seen the video?
Awful.*

HILARY   That video I want it taken off the internet
I don't want anyone else sharing it.

BEN   I don't think that's possible.

HILARY   Of course it's possible.

BEN   It's too late. It's already all over the news.

*Looks like a horror film/poor man/so much
blood/that's awful/tore him to pieces didn't
they?
Didn't agree with a word he said but RIP.
Everyone sharing that neighbour's video of
Cooper's body should have a bit of respect.*

*WATCH: The shocking moment where
Video/footage/footage of Alistair Cooper as*

neighbour finds/shocking/horrible/gross/
awful
D'you wanna watch it?
No of course I don't want to watch it! What
happens in it?
Well, the neighbour is looking over the garden
wall and she's turned her phone on and you
can see this body just lying there outside the
front door and then you can hear a dog
barking because she was walking her dog,
and then you can hear her say ''scuse me,
'scuse me' and she goes down the garden path
and that's when she realises he's dead.
Oh my god.
She films the body, right up close. Everything
is covered in blood seriously, it's awful really
awful. He's been stabbed loads of times and
his stomach is kind of
Jesus. Really?
It's. So awful. Are you sure you don't want to
watch it?

HILARY   You were right. There's no way to take down
that video.
I tried. But it's everywhere.

BEN   Did you watch it? Hilary? Tell me you didn't
watch it.

HILARY   Agnes is going to see it one day.

BEN   Not necessarily.

HILARY   When she's older. I can't stop her. My
daughter will, at some point in her life, watch
a video of her father like. That.

Can't believe people are watching that video.
Anyone watching that video ought to be
ashamed of themselves.
So the woman finds him lying there and
decides to film it for the news? Grim.
She's a vulture.
Parasite.

The neighbour.
The woman who
Emma Watkins, the neighbour of Alistair
Cooper who photographed and filmed his
corpse before calling for an ambulance has
said she regrets sharing the images.

EMMA WATKINS

It was an instinct thing. I took the photos and
the video without thinking. I shared them
because I share everything interesting I take.

Idiot/Stupid woman/What an/Can't believe/I'd
never/Anyone in their right mind would

EMMA WATKINS

Fifteen minutes later I regretted my actions
and deleted my post, but by then it was too
late. The images had gone viral.

Ms Watkins, who along with two other local
residents attended to Mr Cooper before the
arrival of the emergency services revealed
that she had received death threats since the
incident.

EMMA WATKINS

I deeply regret

Disrespectful bitch hope one day you know
what it's like to die like that.

EMMA WATKINS

I deeply regret

I should cut open someone you love and send
the pictures round the world.

EMMA WATKINS

I deeply regret any offence I caused, and my
heart goes out to Mr Cooper's family.

I'm hearing that Emma Watkins has had her
contract terminated by
Woman who shared Cooper footage SACKED
by employer.

> *We are a company that believes*
> *wholeheartedly in empathy and respect for*
> *one's fellow human beings, which is why we*
> *will not be working with Ms Watkins again in*
> *the future.*
> *Good.*
> *Good.*
> *Serves her right.*
> *Hope no one ever employs the silly woman*
> *ever again.*

> *Ali/Alistair/Alistair*
> *Cooper/Coop/Cooper/Alistair*
> *Cooper/Alistai/air Cooper/Cooper/Alistair*
> *Cooper/Alistair Cooper/Alistair Cooper/*
> *Alistair*

BEN	What are you doing?
HILARY	Reading.
BEN	You're searching for Alistair's name?
HILARY	It's interesting. All these people talking about him, talking to him.

> *Cooper/Co/Cooper/Co/Co/Coo/Cooper/*
> *Alistair/Alistair Cooper*

BEN	Why don't you try and get some sleep?
HILARY	I'm fine.
	At the moment it's mostly condolences.

> *My heart goes out to his family.*
> *I hope Hilary Cooper is alright.*
> *What a horrible thing to happen he was*
> *a good principled man that spoke his mind.*
> *RIP.*
> *Love and strength to his family.*

HILARY	But if you go back a few days.

> *I hate Alistair Cooper.*
> *Alistair Cooper is a*
> *I hope Alistair Cooper gets what he deserves.*
> *Awful man.*

Hateful man.
Evil prick.
Ugly bastard.

BEN   I don't think it's healthy to be reading all
               of this.

HILARY   What they're saying. What they said. It makes
               me feel better. People care.

BEN   We still haven't talked about the funeral.

HILARY   There's no point until they release the body.

BEN   Why not turn it off eh?

HILARY   The things they say about him. You tried to
               tell me how bad it was but.
               I had no idea. These people.
               They're monsters.

BEN   Yes. Well. It's hardly surprising.

               That's what happens when

HILARY   What.

BEN   No nothing. You're right. It's disgusting.

HILARY   What?

BEN   He was very good at getting a rise out of
               people. That's all I'm saying.
               He had. There were a lot of people who were
               very angry with some of the things he said.
               Understandably some might say.

HILARY   Are you saying it's his fault?

BEN   No of course not.

HILARY   That he caused this somehow?

BEN   Of course I'm not I just.

HILARY   We don't even know who did it. It could have
               been a mugging a random attack or

BEN   You're absolutely right.

HILARY	They might not have known who he was.
BEN	That's a possibility. Of course. It's just. Unlikely. A lot of people had their issues with him –
HILARY	So he deserved to die?
BEN	No but you can't be surprised when
HILARY	You always hated him.
BEN	That's not true. Just because I didn't agree with him doesn't mean –
HILARY	Maybe it's time you went home.
BEN	Hilary. Come on. You're exhausted.
HILARY	I'm fine. I'd just like you to leave.
BEN	I didn't mean anything by it. I was just.
HILARY	I'd like to be alone with my daughter.
	Can you go now.
	Please.

Alistair Cooper
The murder of Alistair Cooper
Police are investigating leads and are
asking for
Who did it?
Wonder who did it?
How can they not have caught him?
Who is this man? Police release security
footage relating to Alistair Cooper murder.
A man seen to be lurking outside the Cooper
household just hours before he was murdered.
Do you recognise this man? Call this number!

ALISTAIR	Hello, you've reached Alistair Cooper. I'm not available right now but please leave me a message and I'll get back to you.
HILARY	It's. It's me. This is stupid. I don't know why I'm. I just wanted to hear your voice. This is silly. I.

I just. I keep waiting for you to
Nope.
This is stupid.

ALISTAIR   Hello, you've reached Alistair Cooper.

*Manhunt begins for shady figure lurking
outside Cooper residence.
Who is the man in the hat?
We'd be very interested to talk to the person
in this photograph.
Man on security footage revealed to be forty-
two-year-old Mustafa Richards.
Forty-two-year-old local man Mustafa
Richards
British-Turkish man Mustafa Richards.
Turkish man Mustafa Richards questioned by
police over Alistair Cooper murder.
Hilary Cooper
Alistair Cooper's wife Hilary drops two-year-
old daughter Agnes off at a friend's house
Brave Hilary Cooper drops adorable daughter
off at friend's house in pretty blue dress.
Poor little girl.
Aw, that poor little girl. Having lost my own
mum seven years ago I know exactly how
she's feeling.
These pics bring back just how hard it is to
lose a parent. Miss you Dad.
Alistair Cooper's daughter Agnes looks
adorable in little blue dress.
Who is Hilary Cooper: private woman thrust
into spotlight after husband's death.
An exhausted Hilary Cooper takes daughter
to friend's house.
Tired Hilary Cooper.
Exhausted Hilary Cooper.
Poor woman.
Poor woman.
I'm hearing reports
Breaking news
Breaking*

Breaking
Breaking
I'm getting reports that police have arrested
a forty-two-year-old man for the murder of
Alistair Cooper.

BEN   Hi. It's Ben. I saw the news about the arrest.
               Give me a call. I'm worried about you. I'm
               sorry. I never meant to.

               Just give me a call please. Okay.

               Police arrest local man in connection with
               murder of Alistair Cooper.
               WHO IS MUSTAFA RICHARDS? The shady
               life of Alistair Cooper suspect.
               Was Alistair Cooper murder an act of
               terrorism?
               Was Mustafa Richards working under orders?
               Who is behind the murder of Alistair Cooper?
               Apparently he used to send him emails. All
               the time.
               'HI ALISTAIR.' Murder suspect's emails tell
               the tale of a sad, lonely obsession.
               Of all the celebrities to obsess over, imagine
               picking Alistair Cooper.
               Surely that was more than enough grounds to
               declare him insane!

EDITOR   Hilary. It's Paul. Alistair's editor?
               How are you? Everyone at the paper is
               devastated. Just devastated.

HILARY   Thank you.

EDITOR   He was a courageous man. His columns were
               so important to the fabric of the publication.
               We still can't believe it. We're all in shock.

HILARY   Yes. Well.

EDITOR   We were wondering if you'd like to write
               something for us? Maybe something
               celebrating Alistair's work?

HILARY   I. I'm not sure. What would I have to do?

EDITOR   Maybe pick out some favourite recent columns
                   or interviews and write about what he meant to
                   you? We think it could be a lovely way to pay
                   tribute to him. What do you think?

                   *Alistair Cooper murder suspect posted picture
                   of him hours before.*
                   *Cooper suspect posted a picture of him TWO
                   MONTHS AGO.*
                   *Picture of Cooper posted on profile of murder
                   suspect.*
                   *That poor man's daughter got no dad just cos
                   some weirdo took a shine to him.*
                   *I hope that Mustafa Richards is sitting in that
                   cell thinking about Alistair Cooper's wife and
                   daughter.*
                   Look at his eyes. Gives me shivers.
                   *They say he did it with an ordinary kitchen
                   knife.*

5 LIVE PRESENTER
                   Hello you're listening to Radio 5 live. Our
                   topic today: Should there be stricter
                   legislation on who can buy kitchen knives?
                   We want to hear your thoughts.

CALLER   I don't know why more people don't talk
                   about this. My two-year-old can go in and buy
                   a knife from Sainsbury's.

CALLER 2   Knives can kill and I think only those qualified
                   to use them properly and not people who are
                   disturbed should be able to buy them because
                   obviously they are needed instruments but also
                   there's people's lives at stake so yeah.

5 LIVE PRESENTER
                   Okay! Thanks for calling. Let's go to John
                   from Norwich.

                   *Listen to this. What was the last thing to go
                   through Alistair Cooper's head? The knife.*
                   *I heard Alistair Cooper's wife wanted to repaint
                   the front door but he was dead against it.*

*Apparently Alistair Cooper's wife wanted
to repaint the front door but he was dead
against it.*
*What was the last thing to go through Alistair
Cooper's head? The knife.*
*Cooper's wife wanted to repave the garden
but he was dead against it.*
*What was the last thing to go through Alistair
Cooper's head? The knife.*
*Alistair Cooper's wife wanted to repaint the
front door but he was dead against it.*
*Alistair Cooper's wife wanted to repaint the
front door but he was dead against it.*
I don't find that funny.
This isn't something to joke about.
That's disgusting.
Please don't joke about this.
*Here we go, listen to this one. What was the
last thing to go through Alistair Cooper's
head?*
The knife.
Oh you've heard it.

ALISTAIR   Hello, you've reached Alistair Cooper. I'm
not available right now but please leave me
a message and I'll get back to you.

HILARY   Hello. It's me. I know I said this was stupid
but.
I've had a few glasses of. So.
I've been reading your columns. Watching
interviews.
And
They want me to write about you and I want
to but.
I wish you were here so I could ask you.
Did you know what you were doing? Did you
want them to hate you as much as they did?
God I wish you were here.

ALISTAIR   Hello, you've reached Alistair Cooper. Hello,
you've reached Alistair Cooper. Hello, you've

reached Alistair Cooper. Hello, you've
reached Alistair Cooper.

POLICE OFFICER

Ms Cooper. Detective Pinner. There's been
a development in our investigation.

HILARY   What do you mean a development?

*My name is Eric Clarke and I killed Alistair
Cooper.*
*Please let Mustafa Richards go I don't want
an innocent man going to prison for an act
I did.*
This act that I did I did it for all of you.
*I killed him in your name I killed him because
everyone talks and talks about stopping these
people but nobody ever does anything.*

Wow are people seeing this?
Joker.
Wind-up.
Fake.
Obviously fake.
Oh my god.
Can anyone confirm if this is real?

Breaking
Breaking
Breaking news.
Breaking.
Breaking.
*Essex man arrested for murder of Alistair
Cooper after confessing online.*
*Essex man Eric Clarke has been arrested for
the murder of Alistair Cooper after
sensational internet confession.*
Oh my god have you seen this?
Have you seen this?
He confessed online.
Have you read this?
What does he mean 'in your name'?
In whose name? Who's he talking about?

They went straight round and arrested him.
If this was a joke then I bet he's regretting
it now.
That can't be real. That's not real surely.
I'm hearing that in Clarke's house they found
a murder weapon and bloody clothes.
Blood found on Eric Clarke's clothes matches
that of murdered journalist Alistair Cooper.

And I'm hearing
We're getting reports that
Eric Clarke, the man arrested for the murder
of Alistair Cooper, was a long-time
commenter on his articles
Some of Clarke's comments had been reported
for threatening language and questions are
being asked why the Metropolitan Police
didn't investigate sooner.

In a further statement to the police Mr Clarke
said he was acting in the best interest of the
country, and had silenced Alistair Cooper
because it was 'what the people wanted'.

HILARY	'What the people wanted'?
BEN	I'm so sorry.
HILARY	'The best interests of the country.'
BEN	About before. I never meant to –
HILARY	Don't be. You were right.
BEN	Don't say that.
HILARY	I've been going back through Alistair's recent articles. His interviews. Some of the things he's been saying. It doesn't even sound like him. He never used to be like this.
BEN	It's not just him. Everything's getting. Noisier.
HILARY	And now this. So many people hated him.
BEN	You said it yourself. It wasn't the real him.

HILARY   That doesn't matter. He said those things.
Things that made someone so angry they
stabbed him to stop him saying any more.
'What the people wanted.' That's what he said.

BEN   It doesn't matter what he said. He's a madman.

HILARY   I always said I was too busy to read the things
Alistair wrote.
But. Maybe I just didn't want to know.
This man thought it was better to kill him
than to let another one of his opinions out into
the world.

BEN   Look at me. Nobody disagreed with Alistair
more than I did. You know that. He infuriated
me. Pushed every one of my buttons –
something he enjoyed doing by the way.
I remember thinking when you first got
together: 'Oh god, who's this Chino-wearing,
rugby-loving loudmouth and what's he doing
with my sister?' He could be So. Bloody.
Annoying. That first year he came for
Christmas. The Thatcher incident –

HILARY   Mum never forgave him.

BEN   But despite all that, despite his politics and
his brashness and the way he sometimes
spoke to waiters, I liked him. I really did.
He was a good man. Generous. Funny. And
he loved my sister, who loved him back.
You can't blame Alistair for this. No one
could have predicted it. He was just unlucky.

HILARY   Unlucky.

BEN   Listen to me. Whatever he did, said, in his
career. He didn't deserve this. You understand
that, don't you?

*In a post on the forum on 26 March, Clarke
wrote
'Someone needs to silence Alistair Cooper
fast. The longer he's allowed to spout his*

venom the more people will be hurt by the intolerance and hatred he inspires.'
Mustafa Richards released without charge.
Comments underneath Clarke's post included 'completely agree' and 'you go for it mate ha ha'. Police have said they will investigate all those involved in the discussion.

IN YOUR NAME: Killer blames internet hatred for crime.
CONFESSION OF A MURDERER: The internet forum that fostered anti-Cooper hatred.
What do we know about Eric Clarke?

I HATE ALISTAIR COOPER: Eric Clarke's vile posts about murdered journalist.
Some of the things Clarke said about him turn my stomach:

I hate Alistair Cooper.

The man is a hate-filled, black-hearted goblin.

Dear Alistair Cooper. I hate you. Now go away.

Alistair Cooper makes me want to tear my eyes out.

Disgusting.
Some of those Eric Clarke comments about Cooper send a shiver down your spine.
It's amazing that no one picked up on it sooner.

Should Eric Clarke even have been walking the streets?
Cooper murder suspect had been sectioned TWICE.
Well there you go.
Oh dear. Seems like a bit of a weirdo.
Seems like a disturbed man. If only he'd had God in his life.

*Yeah that's just what he needs, more
delusions.
Loner with a history of mental illness.
Can we stop bringing up Eric Clarke's mental
illness as if that's an excuse.
Love how many lefties are talking about this
guy's mental illness it's obvious why he did it.
Bloody social workers softly-softly approach
I mean this was an accident waiting to
happen wasn't it?*

*Hilary Cooper has yet to speak out about her
husband's murder but is said by close friends
to be
His wife still hasn't said anything about
Must be in shock poor woman.*

ALISTAIR   Hello, you've reached Alistair Cooper. I'm
not available right now but please leave me
a message and I'll get back to you.

HILARY   Alistair.
I.
I'm so angry with you.
Why? Why did you have to go that far? Write
those things? Say those things?
You pushed them and pushed them and
pushed them until one of them did this.
Always chasing the biggest possible reaction.
Well here's your reaction. I hope you're happy.
I'm sorry.
I'm here. By myself.
I've got to do this all by myself.
I love you. I miss you so much. I am so angry
with you.

*Whether you agreed with Alistair Cooper or
not this is an attack on free speech.
I don't want to live in a country where we're
afraid
Freedom of speech
Our freedom of speech is threatened by
attacks like this.*

An attack like this is silencing our free/free press is under threat from attacks like these.
Whether you agreed with his politics or not, now's the time to stand together against hatred.
Some of the stuff Cooper said was pretty hateful.
What are you saying, that he deserved to die? The content of his articles is irrelevant. This is an attack on a principle.
Just because he had opinions that some people found difficult.

Can't even imagine what Cooper's wife must be going through right now.

How can he say that he killed Alistair Cooper in our name?
Not in my name mate.
Not in my name.
No, Eric Clarke, you do not speak for me. NotInMyName
Eric Clarke you did not kill him in my name. I did not like Alistair Cooper. But he was an honest principled man and I didn't want him dead.
Some of this violent language that people used about Alistair Cooper is really frightening.
The hypocrisy of some of the people on here who were calling Cooper every name under the sun just a few weeks ago.
I for one never took part in that sort of thing.
'What have we learnt from fallout to the Alistair Cooper murder?'
Totally agree with this.
This article sums up exactly how I feel.
Great read.
Really good read.
Really glad somebody has said this.
Lovely article today John. Getting a lot of traction.

NotInMyName
NotInMyName
NotInMyName
Please share NotInMyName if you disagree
with what Eric Clarke did.
NotInMyName
NotInMyName
Ten reasons why Eric Clarke does not speak
for us all. Please share. NotInMyName.
Please share. Please share.
Dear All. On Thursday there will be a
NotInMyName candlelit vigil in Trafalgar
Square in support of free speech.
No matter his politics, Alistair Cooper was
a great champion of free speech. Let's all
gather in Trafalgar Square to speak for his
legacy.

HILARY   Agnes still doesn't really understand. She knows something's wrong but. I've tried to explain. I don't think it's sinking in.

BEN   You can't expect. At that age.

HILARY   They've asked me to go on the radio to talk about him.

BEN   You know you don't have to if you don't want –

HILARY   No. I want to. There are things that should be said.

Wonderful scenes at Trafalgar Square tonight.
NotInMyName
Wish I could be in Trafalgar Square tonight
looks beautiful.
Wish I could be there.
Would love to be there.

RADIO PRESENTER
     Hilary Cooper, thank you for joining us.

HILARY   Thank you.

So moving.
Really moving.
Tears to my eyes.
Bit self-serving.
In comments that called for moderation and
an end to the language of hatred, Hilary
Cooper condemned the vitriol directed at her
husband

HILARY   It was vicious, hate-filled and at times
downright frightening. And it ended in
his death.

Absolutely right.
Been saying it for years.
It was far too much.
But unexpectedly, she also said that she
wasn't able to defend the tone of her
husband's writing, saying

HILARY   And this is, this is very hard for me to say
because my husband loved his work, I knew
how much it meant to him and he would be
devastated to hear me say this.
But the world needs less Alistair Coopers.

Whoa.
Can't believe she'd write off her husband's
legacy like that.
Less Alistair Coopers? Well there's one less
already.
Saying less Alistair Coopers is a bit
insensitive isn't it?
Doesn't she mean 'fewer'?
Can everyone stop taking her literally.
Wonder what her husband would think about
her saying that.
Her poor daughter.
Kinda sounds like Hilary Cooper is saying he
deserved it.
Poor guy. First he gets stabbed now his wife
trashes his career.

Is it just me who would be at home with my
kids rather than making media appearances.

HILARY   Alistair's death has left a hole in our lives that
can never be filled. It's an indescribable loss.
And I would never say that this was his fault.
But that still doesn't mean he should've said
the things he said.
The only comfort I can find at the moment is
that his death might have an impact beyond
our family, that it might change the way we
talk about the world for the better.

So moving.
Very honest.
I appreciate her honesty.
For her of all people to say that shows how
important this is.
She's absolutely right. There's fault on all
sides.
Heartbreaking.
Beautiful.
The language of hatred needs to stop.
Have we been asking for something like this
to happen?
Anger and hatred have no place in political
discourse.
This can't happen again.
We can't let this happen again.
Tolerance.
More tolerant.
Guys, let's all just be more tolerant.
If I hear one more person talking about
tolerance I think I'm gonna scream.
Let's just have a bit of tolerance for each
other yeah?
I agree.
Absolutely.
I absolutely agree with all of this.
This says what I've been thinking.
Thank god someone finally said it.

*I for one will think twice about the language
I use.*

*Whatever happens, the events of this week
won't be forgotten in a hurry.*

*Alistair Cooper's death will be remembered –
we must not let something like this happen
again.*

*We won't forget the events of this week in
a hurry.*

*We'll be talking about this for a long time to
come.*

*Think we could all learn a lesson or two from
this.*

Lessons learnt.

*The body of Alistair Cooper has been
released to his family for his funeral*

*Alistair Cooper/Alistair Cooper/Alistair
Cooper*

HILARY   The mentions are getting less frequent. People
                aren't writing as much about him.

BEN   I thought you'd stopped reading all that.

                *Alistair Cooper/Alistair Cooper/Alistair
                Cooper/Alistair Cooper/Alistair Cooper/
                Alistair Cooper/Alistair Cooper*

HILARY   I.
                I can't. I know I should but.
                The noise. It's all I've got.
                Everything they're saying about him, good or
                bad. I don't mind any more.
                I want to read it all just so I know I know
                what's happening and in a way it's nice it's
                nice to see his name see his face see the
                whole country talking about him you know
                good or bad it doesn't matter. He would've
                liked it he would've loved it all this talk
                about him.
                Because. So long as they're still talking about
                him it's like he's still here, you know?

And maybe, if his death causes people to change, to make people think twice about the way that they talk about certain things then at least that's something, right?

BEN   Yes. That's something.

HILARY   What I'm worried about is when they stop talking about him.
When it all goes quiet. What happens after that? Because that's when. That's when he'll really be gone.

Alistair Cooper.

Alistair Cooper/Alistair Cooper/Alistair Cooper/Alistair Cooper/Alistair Cooper/ Alistair Cooper/Alistair Cooper/Alistair Cooper/Alistair Cooper/Alistair Cooper/ Alistair Cooper/Alistair Cooper.

Alistair Cooper/Alistair Cooper/Alistair Cooper.

Alistair   Cooper

Alistair   Cooper

Al

The Prime Minister today
Heartless.
The England football team
Prima donnas.
Labour Party members
Morons.
Watch what happens when
Love this
Eugh how awful
Look at this picture of
Idiot
Twenty-three people were killed today in
My heart goes out
So awful
Watch this

Ha ha so good
Heartless bastards
You're disgusting
Stupid set of views
He should be ashamed of himself.
She should be utterly ashamed.
Resign.
Liar!
Everybody should read this now.
So stupid.
Sign this petition.
First.
Spoiler alert.
Thinking of everyone involved in today's
events.
This post has been deleted by the moderators.
Should've been strangled at birth.
Sign this if you care about
Haha this pic just cheered me up.
The man found guilty of murdering Alistair
Cooper was today sentenced to life in prison.
What a wonderful and intelligent article.
Total garbage.
Parasite.
Your response?
Oh I totally agree with this.
More bias
This is awful.
Evil evil people.
Tory rag.
Where do they find these idiots?
This says everything I've been wanting to say
for ages.
Yep.
Totally agree.
Absolutely.
The Prince of Wales
Inbred
Foreign secretary
Idiot

Controversial star
Put some clothes on.
This. One hundred per cent.
Old.
Ugly.
Posh prick.
Scrounger.
Lefty.
Fat cat.
Cheat.
Racist.
Toff.
Smarmy.
Weak.
Hopeless.
Evil.
Fascist.
Stupid.
Idiot.
Idiot.
Oh god not him again.
I hate this guy.
Oh god I hate this guy.
This woman makes me so angry.
I hate him/I hate him/I hate her.
I hate him/I hate them all so much.
I hate her/I hate her/I hate him.

I hate them!

START SWIMMING

48

Acknowledgements

Thanks to Imogen, Rob and all at Young Vic Taking Part.

Our incredible company, and everyone who shared along the way.

And Ola and Tyrell, who made it.

J.F.

Start Swimming was first performed in The Clare, Young Vic, London, on 26 April 2017. The play transferred to Summerhall, Edinburgh, on 2 August 2017, as part of the Edinburgh Festival Fringe. The cast was as follows:

Adrian David Paul
Charlotte Dylan
Eleanor Williams
Emma James
Filipe Caetano
Hana Oliveira
Isaac Vincent
Kaajel Patel
Kimberley Okoye
Kwabena Ansah
Shanice Weekes-Brown

Director & Dramaturg	Ola Ince
Designer	Jacob Hughes
Sound	Max Perryment
Light	Amy Mae
Light (Edinburgh)	Nell Allen
Assistant Director	Tyrell Williams
Production Manager	Emily Seekings
Stage Manager	Annique Reynolds
Assistant Stage Manager	Sophie Rubenstein
Production Stage Manager (Edinburgh)	Viv Clavering
Studio Technician	Nell Allen
Stage Technician	Ryan Smalley
Costume Supervisor	Kinnetia Aisidore
Set	Young Vic Workshop
Participation Project Manager	Rob Lehmann
Director of Taking Part	Imogen Brodie
Young Associate Taking Part	Daniella Connor
Project Assistant	Scarlett Sterne
Marketing Officer	Beanie Ridler

'…so you better start swimming or you'll sink like a stone, for the times they are a-changing'

For Adrian, Charlie, Ellie, Emma, Filipe, Hana, Isaac, Kaaj, Kim, Kwabs, Shanice and Michael

'Disobedience, in the eyes of anyone who has read history, is man's original virtue. It is through disobedience that progress has been made, through disobedience and through rebellion.'

Oscar Wilde

'The definition of insanity is doing the same thing over and over and expecting different results.'

Albert Einstein (probably)

Note on Text

Y indicates an affirmative response – a yes, or a ding, or a reward of some sort.

X indicates a negative response – a no, or a buzzer, or a punishment of some sort.

? indicates a response neither one thing nor the other.

A line with no full stop at the end indicates an unfinished thought.

A dash at the end of a line indicates an interruption.

W

Wo

Whu

Whuuuu

Wha

Wha wha wha wha

Wha wha what.

What?

What.

What ye

What yerrrrrr

What yeeee-errrrrrrrr

Ye-Oooooo

What yoooooo

What you?

D

D

Doeeee

What you doeeee

Ng ng

What you doeeeeeng

H

Ha

Heh

What you doeeing heh.

What you doing here?

Y

What you doing here?

Y

What you doing here?

Y

What you doing here?

Y

I'm?

X

What you doing here?

Um.

X

What you doing here?

I'm.

X

What you doing here?

Breathing?

X

What you doing here?

Blinking?

X

What you doing here?

Sweating?

X

What you doing here?

Standing?

YYYYY

What you doing here?

Standing.

Y

…

X

What you doing here?

Standing.

Why?

X

What you doing here?

Standing.

Where –

X

What you doing here?

Standing. Standing still standing alone standing up standing –

X

What you doing here?

Standing.

You can't stand here.

Y.

Of course I can.

X

What you doing here?

Standing.

You can't stand here. See that sign?

Y

What does it say?

Um.

X

See that sign. What does it say?

Keep off the grass.

Y

And where are you standing?

The grass?

You have to get off.

Y

What if I don't?

Ten-pound fine.

X

One-hundred-pound fine.

Y

I got permission.

From who?

The owner of the grass.

And who's that?

Mr... Grass?

X

What you doing here?

Standing.

On the grass.

That's right.

Well, you're not allowed.

Y

Why?

Because the sign says.

Y

It's bad for the grass.

Y

Bad for the grass? Are my feet poisonous or something? You know how much I spent on these trainers? The grass should be thanking me. I'M SORRY GRASS AM I HURTING YOU ARE MY POISON FEET HURTING YOU?

X

You're being aggressive

Y

How am I being aggressive?

You're being aggressive and talking to me in a threatening manner.

Y

I'm calling the police

Y

Why you got to be like that? I'm just standing on the grass I'm not harming anyone.

The police are on their way. I've given you fair warning.

Y

What'd I do?

X

What did I FUCKING DO?

X

Okay okay okay.

What you doing here?

Standing on the grass.

Y

Why?

I work here...?

Y

I work here.

Why?

It's very well paid and I really enjoy it.

X

It's not that well paid.

Y

But it's flexible.

X

It's not very flexible.

Y

But it involves helping other people and that's really important to me.

X

It's not that well paid.

Y

The hours are awful.

Y

It takes me ages to get there. I don't enjoy it at all.

YY

I don't like my colleagues.

Y

My colleagues don't like me.

Y

I never see daylight.

Y

My feet are covered in blisters. I could be sacked at any time I

Y

I um –

X

What you doing here?

Standing on the grass.

Why?

I work here.

You're fired.

Y

That's not fair.

You were late yesterday.

Y

My train got stuck.

Rules are rules.

YYY

I need this job. Fucksake.

X

Don't swear at me.

Y

I wasn't. I'm sorry.

Y.

I'm looking for a job.

We're closed.

Y

I've got an interview at four-thirty.

It's four-fifty.

Y

I know that. I'm really sorry.

Y

You're twenty minutes late.

My train got stuck.

That's not my problem.

Fucksake.

Don't swear at me.

Y

I wasn't!

X

What you doing here?

Standing. On the grass.

You're not allowed on the grass.

Y

Yeah I know. I'm sorry.

Y

I'm really sorry.

Y

I'm gonna go now.

Y

I wanna go now.

Y

I wanna go now this place isn't what I thought it was.

Y

I wanna go now this place isn't right.

?

I'm standing on the grass but I wanna go now the way these people are looking at me –

?

I'm gonna go now I wanna go now this place isn't what I thought it was. Everything's a bit bookey man. There's a strange smell it's like burnt plastic. All the people seem, the weather is really, and the ground beneath my feet feels all um I'd like to go I'd like to go I'd

XXXX

What you doing here?

Standing.

On the grass.

That's right.

Why?

I don't know.

X

Well, you're not allowed.

Y

Why?

Because the sign says.

Y

Who wrote the sign?

Get off now please.

Y

In a minute.

Now.

Y

If you don't leave I'll have to call security.

Y

I'll leave if you tell me why.

Because you're not allowed on there.

Y

Why?

Because that's the rule.

YYY

Why?

Because it's bad for the grass.

Y

Bad for the grass? Are my feet poisonous or something? I'M SORRY GRASS AM I HURTING YOU ARE MY POISON FEET HURTING YOU?

X

You're being aggressive.

Y

How am I being aggressive?

X

You're being aggressive and talking to me in a threatening manner.

Y

Just wanna know why there's so much grass and I can't even stand on one little bit.

X

I'm sorry. I'll calm down.

Y

I'm calling the police.

Y

Flipsake.

Don't swear at me.

Y

I didn't!

X

I'm sorry.

Y

Don't swear at me I don't need people swearing at me.

Why you got to be like that? I'm just standing on the grass I'm not harming anyone.

X

I've given you fair warning.

What'd I do? What did I FUCKING DO?

X

What's going on?

He's standing on the grass officer.

You're not allowed on the grass sir.

Y

If you'd like to come with me sir. Just to have a chat.

We can chat here.

Let's move it along sir.

Y

That's it. You're under arrest.

Y

Come on. What for?

Resisting arrest.

You're arresting me for resisting arrest? How can you arrest me for resisting arrest?

You're trespassing.

Y

On the grass?

Assaulting an officer.

Y

When did I assault you this is bullshit!

X

Sorry.

Y

How do you find the defendant? Guilty!

Y

I sentence you to one year in prison.

Y

Flippin

Don't swear in court.

Y

I'm sorry.

I'm very sorry for what I did.

Y.

I'm getting out tomorrow.

Get a job.

Y

I'm ready to work.

Y

What you doing here?

I am an incredibly talented hard-working person.

Y

What you doing here?

I have excellent people skills.

Y

I'm punctual. I'm good in a crisis.

Y

I am experienced at using Microsoft Excel.

Y

Microsoft Word. PowerPoint and Outlook.

Y

I'm sorry. What you doing here?

I'm gonna change your life. Seriously. The only reason not to hire me is that it will make your other employees look so shit in comparison that you'll want to get rid of them.

Y

I am the best-looking person who will ever work for you. I will make the most banging playlist for the office party. I will captain all of your company sports teams to league titles.

Y

I will leave the tastiest treats in the staff-room when I come back from holiday. I got the best email banter you have ever read. I can flirt just enough to make people's day a bit brighter but not so much that it crosses into sexual harassment. I will always get the first round in after work. I am the saviour you've been looking for. Seriously take a look at me please look at me look at me give me the job you won't regret it I promise you won't regret it I promise you won't

Y

You're hired!

Yes!

You're fired.

Y

What. Why?

You lied to me.

I didn't lie.

You didn't tell us you had a criminal conviction.

When I tell you what it was for you'll laugh.

We're closed.

Y

I've got an appointment

What time was it?

Four-thirty.

It's four-fifty.

Y

You're twenty minutes late.

Y

If I don't make my appointment that's really bad for me.

Not my problem.

Y

I got rent to pay please.

I'm evicting you.

Y

I'm looking for a job please just give me a couple of weeks
longer.

Can't do it. Sorry.

Y

I'm not going anywhere.

Then I'll have to call the police.

Y

Excuse me sir.

What.

You've been sitting here for three hours and you've only bought a cup of tea.

So?

So other customers might like to use the table.

I'm not doing any harm.

Don't get aggressive with me sir.

Y

I'm not. I wasn't.

Some people have been complaining. About

What?

About the smell.

Come on mate. I've told you before. You can't sleep here.

I'm going.

Y

Come on mate. I've told you before. You can't sleep here.

I'm going.

Y

Come on mate. I've told you before. You can't sleep here.

I'm going.

Y

Come on mate. I've told you before. You can't sleep here. See that sign?

I'm going alright I'm going I'm going I keep going and keep going and keep going but I don't know what I'm supposed to do I don't know what I'm supposed to do –

XXX

Okay.

I got this.

What you doing here?

STANDING.

Y

ON THE GRASS.

Y

BUT I'M NOT ALLOWED ON THE GRASS.

Y

SO I'M GONNA GET OFF RIGHT NOW.

Y

I'M GONNA GET OFF RIGHT NOW AND I'M REALLY SORRY.

Y

I'M GONNA GET OFF RIGHT NOW AND I'M REALLY SORRY I WALKED ON THE GRASS AND I'M GONNA WORK REALLY REALLY HARD AND BE REALLY NICE AND NOT SWEAR AND GIVE LOADS OF MONEY TO THE GRASS CHARITY.

…

I'M STANDING ON THE GRASS BUT I'M NOT ALLOWED
ON THE GRASS SO I'M GONNA GET OFF RIGHT NOW
AND I'M REALLY SORRY I'LL BE GOOD I'LL BEHAVE
AND I WON'T EVER WALK ON THE GRASS AGAIN I
WON'T EVEN LOOK AT SOME GRASS THE WRONG WAY
I WON'T TALK BACK I'LL FOLLOW EVERY RULE I'LL
DO WHATEVER I'M TOLD.

WHATEVER I'M TOLD...

...

HOW IS THAT NOT IT?

Fuck you.

X

Oh you don't like that?

X

Fuck. You.

Fuck you. Fuck you. Fuck you. Fuck you.

XXX

Fuck you. Fuck you. Fuck you. Fuck you. Fuck you. Fuck you.

X

Fuck you. Fuck you. **X** Fuck you. Fuck you. Fuck you. Fuck
you. Fuck you. **X** Fuck you. Fuck you. Fuck you. Fuck you.
Fuck you.

Fuckyou fuckyou fuckyou fuckyou fuckyou fuckyou **X** fuckyou
fuckyou

XXX

Fuckyoufuckyoufuckyoufuckyoufuckyoufuckyoufuckyoufucky
oufuckyoufuckyoufuckyoufuckyoufuckyoufuckyoufuckyoufuck
youfuckyoufuckyoufuckyoufuckyoufuckyoufuck

FUCK YOU!

XXXXXXX

What you doing here?

Standing on the grass.

What does that sign say?

Y

I don't care.

X

Er.

I don't care.

X

What you doing here?

Standing on the grass.

Why?

I want to make a complaint.

X

I want to make a complaint.

X

You'll have to come inside.

Y

No.

X

You'll have to come back tomorrow.

Y

I want to make a complaint.

X

What's the problem?

X

It stinks round here.

X

Nothing to do with me.

Y

There's rubbish all over the streets.

X

I haven't seen any.

Y

The lift in my block doesn't work.

X

I'm sure it does.

Y

I feel sick.

I feel really sick.

Y

Sick to my stomach.

Y

I'm sick of the state of everything and I feel it in my stomach.

X

I'm sick in my stomach and I'm really tired. I'm really tired and I'm sick in my stomach.

X

I'm sick and tired and I'm angry with myself for being so tired I'm angry with myself for being so sick and telling myself it's alright because that's just how we're supposed to feel isn't it that's how we're supposed to feel –

XXXXX

What you doing here?

Grass. Standing.

You're not allowed.

Y

I know that.

Y

So?

So I'm not going anywhere.

X

I'm not going anywhere.

X

Come back tomorrow?

Y

I'm not going anywhere.

X

You can't stay here.

Y

I'm not going anywhere.

X

Come back tomorrow.

Y

I'm not going anywhere.

X

We're closed.

Y

I'm not going anywhere.

X

Get off. Please.

Make me.

X

I'll call the police.

Y

Call them.

X

I'm going to call them.

Y

I want you to call them.

Please just get off.

I'm not going anywhere.

X

What's the problem?

There's dogshit all over my street.

I haven't seen any –

There's dogshit all over my street. The windows on the old
church hall have been broken for two months. **X** There's still a
hole in the pavement from when that lorry hit that tree. The lift
doesn't work. **X** The light on the fifth-floor landing is still
blinking and every time I come home I think I'm in a horror film.
The rubbish isn't being collected on time. No one is taking care
of the public garden. **X** I don't like my neighbours. My
neighbours don't like me. My neighbours shout at me when
I come home. I don't know my neighbours. The baby next door
keeps crying and no one is looking after it. They keep playing
loud music. They keep stamping their feet. **X** They keep putting
shit **X** keep putting shit through my letterbox. The trains don't
run on time. The buses are too full. I can't afford any of the food
round here. There are loads of new people and none of them talk
to me. There are loads of new people and a lot of them look down
when I walk past them. I don't feel welcome in the cafés near my
house. **X** I'm scared to let my dog out because a neighbour's dog
got cut up. My house is too small. It costs too much for me to get

to work. There are too many people with beards. The water is bad for my teeth. You closed the library. **X** You closed the library and now I can't get books out. You closed the library and now I don't have anywhere to go in the afternoons. **X** You closed the library and now I don't have anywhere to use the internet. You closed the library and now there's nowhere to go when it's raining and in case you haven't noticed it rains every single day. There's dogshit all over my shoe just from walking here. There's dogshit all over my fucking shoe and I'm sick of it I'm sick of it I'm sick of it and I'm not going anywhere until you get someone here to start cleaning it off.

XXXXX

What does that sign say?

'Keep off the grass'

Y

And where are you standing?

The grass.

X

Why?

Sign says not to.

X

Why?

Sign said not to.

X

Why?

Because fuck that sign.

X

Fuck that sign and fuck that grass!

X

Fuck that grass and fuck that sign and fuck you too!

XXXX

What you doing here?

Standing on the grass even though I'm not allowed on the grass.

X

Standing on the grass even though I'm not allowed on the grass.

X

I'M SORRY GRASS AM I HURTING YOU ARE MY
POISON FEET HURTING YOU?

X

Standing on the grass and I'm not going anywhere.

X

Not going anywhere.

X

Not going anywhere.

X

I own this lawn.

X

This lawn is mine now.

X

The lawn is a symbol of wealth and oppression.

X

It was designed for lords to show peasants they were richer than
them because they could afford to waste land and the peasants
couldn't.

X

It was designed for the middle classes to show their neighbours
they were better than them because they could afford to waste
time cutting grass and their neighbours couldn't.

X

But we don't have space or time to waste any more so if they're not gonna use it we're going to take it back or rip it up.

X

Rip it up and start again!

X

Take back every lawn around the world.

X

(*Another language*.) *Take every lawn across the world!*

X

I will not get off the fucking grass. This is my grass now.

X

(*In another language*.) This is our grass now.

X

I will stand on the grass for as long as I like.

X

I will stand here for a week.

X

A month.

X

Ten years.

X

I will stand here until I'm ancient and I drop down dead **X** and then my children will stand here until they drop down dead **X** and then their children will stand here until they drop down dead.

X

Move me along and someone else will take my place.

X

We will dance and drink and fuck on the lawn.

X

Set fire to the lawn furniture.

X

Smash the garden gnomes and force-feed them the pieces.

X

We will force-feed them the grass until they are sick.

X

We will pitch a thousand tents.

X

Build houses on the lawn.

X

Houses and streets and pubs and hospitals and libraries and schools.

X

Build a city over every blade of grass and run it so much better than they ever could.

X

We will pave over it. We will pour acid in the soil so nothing grows.

X

We will burn the lawn.

X

Burn the lawn with them still on it.

X

You left us to rot. You sold the grass from underneath us. You stunted our growth. You stopped us before we even got going.

I'm not going anywhere.

X

I'm not going anywhere.

X

I'm not going anywhere.

X

Not going anywhere.

XXXXXXXXXXXXXXXXXXXXXX

XXXXXXXXXXXXXXXXXXXXXXX

XXXXXXXXXXXXXXXXXXXXXX

Hold your ground.

XX

X

Stay strong

X

Keep calm

X

X

X

X

It can't go on forever.

X

X

Stand your

X

Stand your ground

X

X

Be brave!

X

X

X

I can't

X

Hold

X

X

I can't

X

X

X

X

X

X

X

X

ENOUGH. I'm sorry. I can't. What you doing here?

Standing on the grass?

Bang you're dead.

Y

You can't do that.

I'm sorry. Bang!

Y

Stop.

Bang!

Y

Stop that!

Bang! Bang!

YY

You're under arrest.

Y

Fucking hell

X

I'm sorry.

Y

Let's talk about this.

X

No more talking.

Y

I'm going to make you apologise.

X

I'm going to give you a warning.

X

I'm going to hurt you.

X

Kill you.

Y

I'm going to kill you. I'm sorry.

X

I'm going to kill you and I'm not sorry.

Y

Why?

Because I have to.

X

Because someone's told me to.

X

Because it's good for my career.

X

Because I want to make an example of you.

X

Because I want to?

Y

I'm going to kill you because I want to.

Y

Why?

I don't know.

X

It's good for the country.

X

Good for the world?

X

Sends a message.

X

You deserve it?

Y

You deserve it.

Y

Why?

I don't know.

X

You ignored the sign.

Y

You ignored the sign and you walked on the grass.

Y

That's it?

Y

Apparently.

I'm sorry.

X

I'm really sorry.

X

I won't do it again?

X

I'll name names?

X

Too late for that.

Y

I'm going to get started now.

Y

Before you do it. Can I call my mum?

Of course.

X

No

Y

This won't change anything.

Yes it will.

X

This won't change anything.

That doesn't matter.

Y

What you going to do to me?

It's going to be quick.

X

What you going to do to me?

It's not going to hurt.

X

It's going to be very painful.

Y

I'm going to shoot you.

X

Stab you.

X

Torture you.

Y

I'm going to torture you.

Y

I'm going to pull out your hair.

X

Pull out your tongue.

Y

I'm going to pull out your tongue and peel back your nails.

Y

I'm going to pull out your tongue and peel back your nails and rip open your stomach with my hands.

YY

I'm going to. To snap your jaw from its hinges.

Y

What you going to do to me?

Please. No more.

X

I can't.

X

I won't.

XXX

What you going to do to me?

I'm going to peel back your nails **Y** and pull out your tongue and rip open your stomach with my hands and snap your jaw from its hinges **Y** and I'm going to smash what's left of your face over and over and harder and harder until there's nothing left until it's mush and then I'll show that face to the world **Y** and say 'this is what happens this is what happens this is what happens to people like you!'

YYYY

And then I'm going to take your body and string it up over the grass so that no one will ever walk on it again.

X

What more do you want?

X

What more do you fucking want?!

X

I don't understand!

X

X

X

I'm tired.

X

I'm so tired now.

X

No more.

X

I don't care.

X

X

X

X

X

X

X

Standing.

Y

On the grass.

I'm standing on the grass and trying to change the world
before –

X

I'm standing on the grass and trying to change the world but
I don't think I can change the world.

Y

And because I want to change the world but I don't think I can
change the world I'm going to get off the grass

Y

And go buy fair-trade candles and organic avocados and I'll
take photos of them. And then I'll meet someone and I can take
photos of them instead on holiday or out for brunch and I can
ask them to move in with me and we can find a shit flat that we
don't like in a part of town we never wanted to live in and then
we can get married so there are more photos we can take and
when we get bored again we can have a child and there'll be
even more photos to take and then everything might be alright

because I can pin all my hopes on my child instead and be okay with the fact that I'm not going to change the world because maybe I can be the parent of someone who changes the world and that's good enough for me my child could be Prime Minister or lead a revolution or cure cancer or some other horrible disease although if it's Prime Minister everyone will hate it and if it leads a revolution it will probably die or kill lots of people or both and if it cures cancer everyone will love it at first but then after a while people will stop dying and everyone will live to a really old age and they'll probably use robots or something to take the cancer cure and use it to create a cure for death itself which means that nobody dies of natural causes which means that there's too many people which means that there's no room the air is stale everything stinks there aren't any jobs there are no new ideas dictators live on and on and on the worst wars in human history break out over who gets to have my child's cure mothers don't remember giving birth to their children nobody takes any risks everybody just sits in their chair because they're afraid of dying from an accident when they could live forever and I don't want that I don't want that to happen but there's another part of me that thinks that whatever I do in my life whether I'm good or bad have a child or live alone get a job that I love or a job that I hate whether I try and help other people or only look out for myself or even if I do somehow manage to change the world for a while it doesn't really matter because no matter what we do things always go back the same way and whatever I do I'm going to end up in the same place with no mind and no memories no memories of anything and my body is going to be burnt up there won't be anything to prove that I ever existed so what's the point of even living at all because if time is infinite then there's no real difference between dying at my age and dying at one hundred if anything it's better to die now less pain less anger less stress less confusion less confusion less confusion less confusion less confusion less confusion but then when I think about dying –

When I actually think about dying –

Y

What's the point?

What's the point in even – ?

There's nothing for me here any more.

XXXXXXXXXXXXXX

What you doing here?

What you doing here?

What you d–

No.

Let's just.

I'm not going anywhere.

I'm not going anywhere.

I'm not going anywhere.

I'm not going anywhere.

I'm not going anywhere.

I'm not going anywhere.

I'm not going anywhere.

I'm not going anywhere.

I'm not going anywhere.

I'm not going anywhere.

I'm not going anywhere.

I'm not going anywhere.

I'm not going anywhere.

I'm not going anywhere.

I'm not going anywhere.

I'm not going anywhere.

I'm not going anywhere.

I'm not going anywhere.

I'm not going anywhere.

I'm not going anywhe

I'm not going anyw

I'm not going any

I'm not going an

I'm not going a

I'm not going

I'm not goin

I'm not goi

I'm not go

I'm not g

I'm not

I'm not

I'm not

I'm no

I'm no

I'm no

I'm

I

I

I

I

A

Ahuh

Ayeh

Iee
Ieeeeeee
Aye.

I.

I

I

Ieeeeeeeeeeeooooooooommmm m m m m m

Ieeeeeeeeeem Ey-um. Eyeeeum.

I'm. I'm.

Mmhm.

I'm nnnnnnnnnnnnnn. Nnnnnnnnnnnnaaaaa.

I'm

Nnnnnnnnnnnnnnooooooooo. No no no no. I'm n not.

I'm. N not. Guh. Guh. Guuuuuuuuoo. Guoiii.
Guuuuuuuuooooooooiiiiiii

I'm. Not. Guhooooooiiiiiii. Goeeeeeen. Goeeeen.

Ey-um n not Gooen guh. Goeeeing.

Any

Any

Any wuh

Any wuooooh

Any wuh wuh wuh

Any wuh ey

Ey-um n no goiing any wheee

Any w-air

Anywhere

I'm not goiiing anywuh

Anywuuuu

Anyweeooo

Oh.

Ngh.

Ngh!

I'm nnnnooooot goiiing aneeeeee

Aneeeee

Anywhere! I'm not going anywhere!

**I'MNOTGOINGANYWHEREI'MNOTGOINGAN
YWHEREI'MNOTGOINGANYWHEREI'MNOTG
OINGANYWHERE!**

What does that sign say?!

Keep off the grass!

And where are you standing?

The grass.

Y

Young Vic Taking Part

About Young Vic Taking Part

Our work with young people and all those in our neighbourhood is a major part of our artistic life.

Taking Part engages with over 15,000 people a year. We offer young people and our neighbours free tickets to all our shows. We also run a wide range of projects, from skills-based workshops to opportunities to perform on one of our stages.

To find out more about our projects and how you can get involved, please visit **www.youngvic.org/taking-part www.twitter.com/yvtakingpart**